Please return or renew this item before the latest date shown below

Scottish Inventors

Scottish Inventors

Gary Smailes

Illustrated by Scoular Anderson

BIRLINN

For Anna and Zoe

First published in 2011 by
Birlinn Limited
West Newington House
10 Newington Road
Edinburgh
EH9 1QS

www.birlinn.co.uk

ISBN: 978 1 84158 930 5

British Library Cataloguing-in-Publication Data
A catalogue record for this book is available from the British Library

Typeset by Iolaire Typesetting, Newtonmore
Printed and bound by Grafica Veneta S.P.A., Italy

Contents

Introduction

Over the centuries, famous Scots have earned their place in history for many things . . . there have been great sportsmen, brave explorers and even vicious warriors. But in this book you will meet a different set of famous Scots, a group of people who are famous for the thing that matters most – their ideas.

So enter *Scottish Inventors*. This book brings you the little guys with big ideas. They aren't kings and queens, but ordinary people who had a burning desire to create stuff that would improve the world around them. All the people in this book have one thing in common – they invented something worth remembering. Some of the inventions were earth-shattering, changing the way you and I live today. Some were simple and have passed by with little more than a brief mark in history. And some were just silly, mentioned here to bring a smile to our faces.

1

Transport

Scottish inventors are a creative lot, always cooking up one thing or another. Some of these inventions have been small and insignificant, passing in the blink of an eye. But others have been huge, the type of thing that knocks your socks off and changes forever the way you live.

So, to kick off our parade of famous Scottish inventors, let's start with one of the all-time greats – James Watt.

James Watt:
Making Things a Little Bit Better

When James Watt set about inventing in the 1700s, steam was the big thing. People were obsessed with using steam to power anything and everything – steam-powered trains, steam-powered cars, steam-powered dogs (not really). James Watt is a very famous Scottish inventor – we are talking David Beckham famous here – so there has been lots written about him. The problem is that much of what has been written is boring. And I mean REALLY boring.

However, here are a few interesting facts about the young Watt:

- **He didn't go to school:** Watt was a sickly boy and spent most of his childhood confined to his bedroom. His mother would teach him during the day. Can you imagine what it must have been like for the poor boy? Not only was his mum his teacher, but he was taught in his own bedroom with no way to escape!

- **He liked poetry:** As a young boy Watt would tramp across the hills near his grandparents' home, reciting poetry to anyone unlucky enough to pass by.

- **He liked to take his toys apart:** Watt had only a few toys, but those he did own he would regularly take apart and rebuild.

- **He was banned from sport:** When Watt finally went to Greenock Grammar School his teachers decided he was too weak and girly to play sport. In fact, the only sport he ever showed any interest in was angling, which I am not even sure is a sport.

Watt wanted to become an engineer, but very few people took him seriously. So, he moved to Glasgow and set up a workshop in the university. His job was to help the professors keep their inventions and machines in working order.

OK, here's the tricky bit that might upset a few stuffy historians . . .

James Watt is famous for one thing – inventing the steam engine.

But that's just not true.

The first working steam engine was invented by Thomas Newcomen. It was like a giant kettle, using boiling water to produce steam, which, when released, would move a piston up and down and this would help turn the steam into power. Glasgow University had its own Newcomen steam engine, and Watt looked after it before ever working on his own machine.

So what's what with Watt?

Well, he never claimed to have invented the steam engine. But he did make it a little bit better. It was all to do with the way the steam was produced and captured, and the use of condensers (which convert steam into water). It's pretty boring stuff but all you need to know is that Watt took Newcomen's design and made it better. Watt was the guy who made the first steam engine that was cheap enough and safe enough to be used in factories and mines.

One thing Watt did that was really clever was partnering up with Matthew Boulton (who had loads of cash) and setting up a company to sell steam engines. Their steam engines sold very well, especially to tin mines in Cornwall, where they were used to power pumps to remove water from the deep shafts. However, the steam engines had one big problem. They could blow up! Steam could also leak from the pipes, stopping the machine from working altogether.

These problems kept Watt awake at night. He would toss and turn in bed trying to think of something he could use to stop the leaks. He tried just about everything including corks, rags soaked in oil, old hats, newspaper and even horse dung!

Watt was asked to build an engine to be used in London. It was called The Bow. When the huge engine was installed, its new owner was so impressed that he gave Watt's workman a gift of money. Unfortunately, when the workman took a break, he went straight to the pub, spent the money on beer and returned to the engine roaring drunk. He turned The Bow on and left it running at full blast. Steam rushed through the pipes, bursting valves and springing leaks. It cost Watt a fortune to fix the damage.

Despite their problems, Watt's steam engines were still the envy of the world. It was not long before foreigners were poking around his workshop. Germany and France sent spies to try to bribe Watt's workers to reveal the secrets of cheap and safe steam engines. The Russians went

one better, sending the wife of the Tsar, the Empress of Russia. She was so amazed by Watt's steam engines that she wanted to stay an extra day to examine them further. She hadn't made arrangements for this and had nowhere to stay. In the end she stayed overnight at Boulton's house!

In 1781 Watt started to experiment with the idea of using a steam engine to power a carriage on the road. He filled numerous notebooks with sketches of possible designs. For the carriage to work it would need the steam to be pumped at very high pressure. This was dangerous and could easily lead to explosions. Watt refused to take the risk but one of his employees, who we'll come to next, was a little bolder.

William Murdoch:
The Man behind the Man

The secret to James Watt's success was not Watt's amazing mind or his ability to keep going no matter what. It was the people he got to help him. One of Watt's best men was a Scot called William Murdoch.

Murdoch was born in Lugar near Cumnock, East Ayrshire, in 1754 (he later changed his name to Murdock to make himself sound more English, but we will have to forgive him for that!). As a young boy he loved to invent things. In fact, he had his own inventing cave near the River Lugar. He was a bit like a Scottish Batman with his cave full of gadgets and new inventions!

William Murdoch was a strange kid. Whilst still at school, he helped his dad to invent a three-wheeled bike that was powered by hand-driven pistons (described as a 'wooden horse on wheels'), and he even helped to build a bridge over the River Nith.

When Murdoch was in his twenties he heard of Watt's company and its reputation for making amazing machines. Murdoch really wanted to work with Watt, so he walked the 300 miles from his home to Watt's office, just to ask for an interview. When he arrived, he was told that there were no jobs. Murdoch was about to leave when Matthew Boulton saw Murdoch's strange hat. He had made the

hat himself, fashioning it from wood with a machine called a mechanical lathe. Boulton was so impressed by his fine craftsmanship that he offered Murdoch a place in the company.

Murdoch quickly proved his worth – he was not only a great engineer but also a good leader.

One story tells of trouble Watt was having with a group of Cornish miners who were bullying Watt's workmen. Murdoch travelled to the mine to talk to the bullies. He asked the troublemakers to meet him in a room, and when they all entered Murdoch slammed and locked the door.

'Now then, gentlemen,' said Murdoch. 'You shall not leave until we have settled matters once and for all.'

A fight broke out and after Murdoch had knocked the biggest bully out cold, they all shook hands and the miners went back to work, never again to cause trouble!

Murdoch might have worked for Watt but he continued to invent stuff all his life. Here's a list of some of his more unusual inventions:

- **Air-powered message tubes:** A message would be written and placed in a small container. This was pushed into a long tube and compressed air was used to fire it along the tube. Harrods in London used the system in the 1940s, and it was widely used right up to the 1970s.

Message received!

- **The steam cannon:** Murdoch developed a cannon powered by steam. In 1803 he used the cannon to knock down a wall.
- **The steam gun:** Murdoch also designed a steam-powered gun, which could fire a 3-centimetre-long lead bullet.

However, Murdoch's most famous inventions were a steam-powered car and gas lighting.

Steam-powered car

In 1784 French engineer Nicolas-Joseph Cugnot made a steam-powered car. Murdoch thought he could improve on the design, but James Watt was still worried about exploding steam engines and tried to stop Murdoch from making a new steam-powered car.

Murdoch ignored Watt and went on to make the first British car ever to move on its own. It was a three-wheeled vehicle with a large steam tank on the back (a bit like a big kettle). Murdoch's steam car bore more than a passing resemblance to the three-wheeled bike he and his dad had built all those years before.

Some books will try to tell you that Murdoch, who had stayed on in Cornwall, would travel from mine to mine in his steam-powered car. Unfortunately, this is not true (though it would have been cool). The roads at the time were muddy tracks and simply far too bumpy for a steam-powered car.

Gas lighting

Murdoch was not only obsessed with steam – he loved gas too. In 1792 he started to experiment with using gas to light the lamps in houses. At the time there was no electricity and lamps were fuelled by oil, which was expensive, smelly and dirty, and often made from whale fat!

In 1794 Murdoch ran piping through his house in Redruth, Cornwall, and it became the first house in Britain to be lit by gas.

William Murdoch even made a gas lantern to show him the way home on dark nights. A written report from the time tells us that Murdoch filled a bag with gas (called a 'bladder'!), placed it under his arm, and squeezed it 'like a bagpipe', which sent out a stream of gas to light his lantern.

Henry Bell: Full Steam Ahead

Henry Bell was born at Torphichen, near Bathgate, in West Lothian, in 1767. By the time he was a young man he was already well educated as a ship designer. If you wanted to travel anywhere by boat during the 1700s you had two options – you could roll your sleeves up and row, or you could pop up a sail and let the wind take you. Bell was convinced that there was a third option – steam power.

He wrote to the British government and even to Admiral Nelson, trying to convince them that steam ships were the future. When no one took him seriously, he wrote to the American government. No luck there either.

In 1808 Bell moved to Helensburgh, on the north shore of the Firth of Clyde. It was the perfect time to prove his ideas were more than just hot air (See what I did there? Steam is hot air, talking rubbish is said to be hot air, they are both hot air . . . oh, never mind!). By 1812 his pride and joy was built, and he was able to reveal to the public a steam ship that would take passengers between Glasgow and Greenock. He called the ship *Comet*.

The *Comet* was a success and passengers flocked from miles around to sail in the world's first steam-powered passenger ship. Bell was able to expand his service, taking more passengers and sailing to more places.

Then disaster struck in 1820. On the day in question, the ship set out in bad weather. At first all was well, but as the weather worsened the *Comet* became caught in strong currents and sank at Craignish Point, near Oban.

Bell was not a man to be put off by a little thing like a sunken ship and set about building a second ship, which he called . . . *Comet II* (I bet he was up all night thinking up that name).

So what do you think happened to *Comet II*? A long and successful life as a passenger ship? No . . . just five years after it was built, *Comet II* sank after hitting another boat. Sixty-two passengers were drowned. The disaster was just too much for Bell. Losing ships was one thing, but the deaths of 62 passengers was another. Bell gave up and never built another ship.

Thomas Telford: He Liked a Good Bridge

Watt, Murdoch and Bell were certainly great Scottish inventors. Their work was so important, their names are known all over the world. Before we move on to some Scots whose ideas are less well known, let's look at another super-famous Scot.

Thomas Telford was born in 1757, on a small farm in Eskdale, Dumfriesshire. As a child he was always building things, and at the age of 12 he became a stonemason. The first big project he was involved in was a stone bridge crossing the River Esk in Langholm.

When he was older he moved to London. He taught himself more about building, eventually taking charge of large building projects.

So what makes Telford a great inventor?

That's a good question. Let's start by showing why Telford was a great builder. The bridge at Langholm was one of the first things he ever built. And he just kept building bridges, lots of bridges, and I mean lots! Here's a list to prove the point:

Bannockburn Bridge, Bewdley Bridge, Bonar Bridge, Bridgnorth Bridge, Bridge of Keig, Broomielaw Bridge, Buildwas Bridge, Cantlop Bridge, Chirk Aqueduct, Clachan Bridge, Conwy Suspension Bridge, Coundarbour Bridge, Craigellachie Bridge, Dean Bridge, Dunkeld Bridge, Eaton Hall Bridge, Galton Bridge, Glen Loy Aqueduct, Holt Fleet Bridge, Longdon-on-Tern Aqueduct, Menai Suspension Bridge, Montford Bridge, Mythe Bridge, Over Bridge, Pontcysyllte Aqueduct, Potarch Bridge, Telford Bridge, Tongland Bridge and Waterloo Bridge at Betws-y-Coed.

But Telford was a man of many talents. He helped re-build Shrewsbury Castle, Shrewsbury Prison, the Church of St Mary Magdalene at Bridgnorth and another church in Madeley. He also had a go at building canals and constructed a canal that linked Wrexham in North Wales with Chester, and also a town in Shropshire called Ellsmere. Canals were really important because they made it easy to move things like cloth and coal around the country. Telford's canal was hundreds of miles long in total, plus he built a few bridges along the way (did I mention that he liked bridges?).

Next, Telford decided to build a road. However, he didn't like small challenges, he liked to think big. The road he built stretched all the way from London to Holyhead in North Wales. In the end, he built more than 1,000 miles of road . . . which included a few more bridges.

This is all great, and Telford was certainly a busy man, but what did he actually *invent*? Well, the answer is . . . a lot. Telford was always coming up with ingenious ways to solve problems, whether it was using new material like iron or unusual designs like his circular arch on the Bannock-burn Bridge. Here are two more things Telford invented:

- **Sticky stuff:** In 1805 Telford was in the process of building his Wrexham to Ellsmere canal. However, he had a problem at Pontcysyllte. The canal needed to cross a large valley, so Telford needed a bridge. He drew up plans to use iron panels to create a kind of channel and mount this high above the valley. The water would flow along the iron channel and narrow boats would sail across. The problem was that the iron panels leaked! Telford tried all sorts of material to stop the leaks and, in the end, had to invent his own sticky solution. The answer? Boiled sugar mixed with lead. He used the concoction to seal all the leaky joints.

- **Black stuff:** When Telford agreed to build the road from London to Holyhead, he knew he faced a big problem. At the time, the way roads were being made was pretty much the same as the way the Romans had built them. This meant using layers of big blocks – fine, if you are marching an army, but not a hard-wearing surface for heavy carts and carriages to travel on. So Telford being Telford, he came up with a new system. He looked at each stretch of road, worked out how heavy the traffic would be and then used a collection of specially selected broken rocks to build the road.

This produced a smoother and more stable road surface. In fact, this was the way roads would be built until another Scottish inventor, John Loudon McAdam, who we'll come to next, had his say a few years later.

Thomas Telford never really stopped building and inventing. Even as he grew older he continued to be involved in major engineering projects, such as the redevelopment of St Katharine Docks in London. He died in 1834 after an illness. He was given a huge funeral in Westminster Abbey.

John Loudon McAdam:
King of the Black Stuff

Thomas Telford was the first man to have a crack at improving the way roads were built in Britain. The second man to improve those roads was Scottish inventor John McAdam.

John McAdam was born in Ayr, and was the son of the Baron of Waterhead. McAdam moved to New York, America, in 1770, made his fortune as a businessman, and returned to Scotland in 1783, filthy rich.

He was at a loose end when he returned to Scotland and decided to pass the time as a trustee for Ayrshire Turnpike. His job was basically to look after the roads in Ayrshire. He

Too many potholes! Not good!

enjoyed his new work and after a few years moved on to bigger things, taking a job to look after the roads in Bristol, in south-west England.

McAdam became convinced that people were building roads in the wrong way. In fact, on three separate occasions he sent reports to Parliament, explaining that a new method of road building was needed. In 1816 he got sick

of waiting for the government to act and decided to alter the roads in Bristol himself. He started by using crushed stone (Telford's idea) and building roads with a camber (this means they are higher in the centre and slope out to the left and right) to allow water to drain off.

However, McAdam's biggest and best invention was . . . (take a deep breath and have a go at saying it!) 'macadamisation'. This involved mixing small stones with black, sticky tar. When left to set, the solid roads were smooth and waterproof. The tar mixture was called 'tarmac' (or tarmacadam – Tar McAdam, see what they did there?), hence 'macadamisation'.

John McAdam died in 1836, during a trip home to Scotland. His invention is still used to build roads today. Just look at the nearest road. See? I bet it's black and curved and made of tarmac.

Kirkpatrick Macmillan: The First Bike and perhaps the First Bike Accident . . .

We have seen steam-powered cars, lots of bridges and super-smooth roads, but when it came to getting around the high roads and low roads, the Scots of old loved a good bike. It turns out Scottish inventors played a big part in the invention of bikes. It's just not all that clear who invented what!

Kirkpatrick Macmillan was not your average child. Born and brought up in Dumfriesshire, in 1824 he saw a man riding a bike known as a Hobby Horse. This was simply two wooden wheels and a wooden seat.

It had no pedals, meaning that the rider had to push it along with his feet. Not very fast, not very comfortable, and on a bumpy road the rider was certain to end up with a very bruised bum!

Macmillan really wanted a Hobby Horse. His dad had more sense and said no, so Macmillan still set about building his own. He was soon clattering along the country lanes near his house on his homemade Hobby Horse, but Macmillan wanted more – he felt the need for speed. He quickly worked out that if he could find a way to make the bike move without pushing the ground with his feet it would go faster. So, after tinkering about in his dad's blacksmith's workshop, the young Scot was able to magic up a basic pedal system.

The bike was heavy and the pedals were difficult to use, but Macmillan quickly mastered it and soon he was making the 14-mile journey from his house to Dumfries – in less than an hour!

Macmillan had even bigger plans. In June 1842, then a fully grown man, he set off on an epic 68-mile trip to Glasgow. The ride took two days and must have left Macmillan with the sorest bum in Scottish history!

On arriving in Glasgow our brave adventurer found that there were many more people walking the streets than he was used to in his home town. People stopped and stared, and he had to weave in and out of them, making it difficult to control his contraption. Travelling at 8 miles per hour, and unable to stop, Macmillan collided with a small girl, knocking her over. The girl was OK, with only a few scrapes and bruises, but the police were not impressed and our hero was sent to court and fined five shillings. Believe it or not, legend tells us that the judge was so impressed by the bike that he paid the fine himself in return for a ride!

The journey back was eventful too. As Macmillan raced through the country lanes on his homemade bike, he came upon a horse-drawn stagecoach and decided to race it! His legs were a blur as he pushed the pedals faster and faster, and he soon pulled ahead of the coach, to the amazement of those travelling inside.

Our hero was never interested in making money from his invention and it was soon being copied by others. For many years Gavin Dalzell of Lesmahagow was believed by many to have invented pedal-powered bikes, though eventually Macmillan was given the credit. Our hero died in 1878, and a plaque can still be found outside his family home, which reads 'He builded better than he knew'. Today Kirkpatrick Macmillan's bike is on display in the Glasgow Transport Museum.

Thomas McCall: Looking Backwards

There was another ingenious Scot who wanted to get in on the act of bike-building. His name was Thomas McCall. He was born in the village of Penpont, in south-west Scotland, in 1834, but moved to Kilmarnock at the age of 20.

In 1869 he built a new type of bike. What made McCall's bike different from the other bikes of the time was that it was powered by levers attached to the *back* wheel. The rider would push down on the levers, causing the back wheel to turn. Before this, bikes had always had levers attached to the front wheel.

So, Macmillan invented pedal-powered bikes and McCall built the first bike to be powered by the back wheel. Seems pretty clear . . . right?

Well, maybe. It turns out that McCall might have copied his design. McCall built replicas of bikes he had seen in the past. It is probably the case that McCall wasn't trying to cheat, he just wanted to build bikes and did this by copying other designs. It was later on that historians started to call him an inventor.

Robert Thomson and John Boud Dunlop:
The Saviours of Bruised Bums

I am not saying that Scots have delicate bums, or are afraid of the odd bump or two in the road, but it was not long after the invention of the bike that the solution to a more comfortable ride came along.

The saviour of bruised bums was Robert Thomson. He was born in 1822 in Stonehaven, Aberdeenshire. Thomson was an argumentative young boy and when he left school at 14 he travelled to America to be an apprentice in his uncle's merchant business. He didn't last long and was soon sent back to Scotland, where he taught himself chemistry, electricity, astronomy and mathematics.

In 1846 Thomson invented a new type of tyre. Before Thomson's invention, bike wheels were coated in metal or wood. This made the bike very uncomfortable to ride, with every pot hole in the road jerking and bashing the bike frame . . . and the rider.

Thomson's tyre was made from a hollow, rubber tube that wrapped around the wheel frame. This was then filled with air, providing a much more comfortable ride. It was called a 'pneumatic' tyre. The problem was that the technology at the time didn't allow the rubber tube to be made as thin as was needed for bike tyres. The only tyres that could be made were thick and chunky. Thomson did fit a few of his pneumatic tyres to horse-drawn carriages, but although they worked well they didn't really catch on.

It wasn't until 43 years later, when fellow Scottish inventor John Dunlop arrived on the scene, that pneumatic tyres finally took off.

John Dunlop

John Dunlop worked as a vet. One day in 1887, he was looking to improve his young son's tricycle. As with all bikes at the time, the ride was bumpy and uncomfortable. Dunlop came up with the idea of a tyre made from rubber and – you guessed it – filled with air. He tried it and when it worked he set about making more that he could sell. A year later he was told by the Patent Office (the people who keep a record of inventions) that Robert Thomson had already invented the pneumatic tyre. Dunlop had used new technology to solve the problem of using thick rubber, but the air-filled tyre had already been invented.

Despite the bad news, Dunlop continued to develop the tyre, and in 1890 he went into partnership with a politician and businessman called William Harvey Du Cros. The tyre was a success, but because Dunlop couldn't claim to have invented the pneumatic tyre he never really made much money from it.

2

Communication

I don't want you to think that Scots are only interested in inventing new ways to get around. In fact, some of the greatest Scottish inventors ever have dedicated their lives and brains to trying to making it easier to talk and stay in touch. It is for this reason that we now turn our attention to communication.

John Anderson: Full of Hot Air

Postmen are great, with their big bags of letters, rickety bikes and black-and-white cats. But just imagine how much cooler postmen would be if they delivered your mail by hot-air balloon. This was the dream of John Anderson. Actually, that is a bit of a lie. Anderson never imagined postmen sailing down your street in hot-air balloons, but he was serious about mail being transported by balloon.

Anderson was born at Rosneath, in Argyll and Bute, in 1726. He was a clever man and became a professor at the University of Glasgow. Our hero was full of good ideas. He was the first person in Glasgow to install a lightning conductor and he encouraged James Watt (remember him?) to develop his steam engine. In 1791 he even invented a new type of cannon.

I'll have to hurry and get this thing finished!

Though all of this is pretty cool, it is for his balloons that we will remember Anderson. He was a big supporter of the poor and when the French Revolution began in 1789, he was all for chopping off the heads of the rich aristocrats. Germany, right next-door to France, was worried that its people would get ideas about rebelling too, and stopped French newspapers from being sold in the country. Anderson came up with a great idea to smuggle French newspapers into Germany – balloons!

John Anderson suggested that individual balloons be filled with a type of gas, called hydrogen, and a newspaper attached. The balloons could then be released to float across the border into Germany. The French rebels thought it was a great idea and sent off hundreds of balloons.

So, was Anderson's idea clever or a bit silly? Well, his idea never really took off (took off . . . see?). One problem was that hydrogen-filled balloons tended to explode. A solution to this problem is to use balloons filled with helium (the gas that makes your voice all squeaky). Helium balloons can actually travel great distances. In fact, in 2008, Oskar Haberlandt released a helium-filled balloon in Austria and it floated all the way to Russia!

All the same, I can't see the Royal Mail delivering letters by balloon in the near future. But it would be cool.

James Chalmers: Sticking to His Idea

Here's another Scottish inventor who wanted to make his mark on the great British postal service.

James Chalmers was born in Arbroath, Angus, but moved to Dundee in 1809. He set up a small business on Castle Street, selling books as well as printing and publishing a newspaper. Chalmers was a popular and powerful man in Dundee.

There was one thing that got Chalmers really hot under the collar – the rubbish postal service. In 1825 he started a campaign to speed up the mail service between Edinburgh and London. He wanted it to be faster, but no more expensive. He wrote letters and gave speeches explaining just how they could make it faster. In the end, the postal service listened, tried his ideas and cut down the delivery time by a full day.

Your mail, Mr. Chalmers!

So far so good. But in 1837 Chalmers still hadn't calmed down and he came up with yet another improvement to the postal service – the stamp. Chalmers' idea was for a stamp that could be stuck to an envelope to show the postage had been paid.

Chalmers died in 1853 and was never really been credited with inventing the sticky stamp.

Why not?

Well, it's not a simple question to answer. At the time, if you lived in London it was possible to send parcels and letters using the London Penny Post. This was a system that saw the parcel or letter stamped with a mark to show you had paid. Not really a sticky stamp though.

Chalmers was not the only person in the UK who wanted to improve the postal system. In 1835 an Englishman called Sir Rowland Hill published a book all about changing the system. Hill even talked to the government about the idea of using a sticky stamp. In the end it was Hill's ideas that were used.

A few books have been written suggesting it was our hero, James Chalmers, who first came up with the idea of the sticky stamp. This might be true, but history can be cruel, and it is Sir Rowland Hill who usually gets the credit.

Alexander Graham Bell:
Great Inventor or Thief?

Now we come to one of the biggies . . . the telephone.

False heads and talking dogs

Alexander Graham Bell was born in Edinburgh in 1847. His mother suffered from growing deafness and, as she became harder of hearing, Bell learned the best way to be understood was to speak clearly. As things got worse he learned a sign language so they could communicate. In fact, Bell became a bit obsessed with communicating, experimenting with the loudness and tone of his voice, to see which was best heard by his mother.

I SAID, CAN YOU HEAR ME, MOTHER?

Bell's dad was also a big influence. He was an expert in writing down the sounds of speech. Think about it, can you write down what words actually sound like? It's pretty tough. Bell's dad developed his own language to do just this and taught it to Bell.

In 1863 all of Bell's passions came together. His father took him to see a display of mechanical heads that could mimic the sound of speech. Bell was fascinated and bought the book that explained how to make a talking head. But it was written in German. So Bell simply learned German, translated the book, and built his own speaking machine!

Our hero now turned his attention to his pet dog. He started by teaching the dog to growl with a steady note. The next step was to train the dog to move its lips and mouth to match certain sounds. By the time Bell had finished, the dog could clearly say, 'How are you, grandma?'

Sound and wires

In 1870, when Bell was 23, his family moved to Canada and he set up a workshop at their new farm. He continued to experiment with sound. After taking a job teaching at a deaf school, Bell continued his work on what he called his 'harmonic telegraph'. He wanted to send sound along a wire by altering pitch (this is how fast the sounds vibrate, a bit complicated but all that you need to know is that Bell was trying to make sound move down a wire). His aim was to change sound into electrical pulses at one end, send these pulses down the wire, and convert them back to sound at the other end. The problem was that the device used to turn the pulses back to sound wasn't complete and needed a lot more work.

Watson and telephones

By 1874 Bell was making progress. He had improved the way sound was being captured. He was also able to send this captured sound down a long wire. However, he was unable to convert it back into sound at the other end. The best he could manage was a machine that would trace the shape of the waves. Nice to look at, but pretty useless.

Bell didn't understand enough about electricity to convert the electrical pulse back into sound. This all changed when he met Thomas Watson. He was an experienced designer of electrical machines and was happy to work with Bell.

The new partnership quickly developed and within a few months they had cracked the sound problem. Though they had not yet invented the telephone, they had invented a system that allowed sound to be transmitted through a wire and 'heard' at the other end.

Patents and cheats

Up until this point the story has been pretty straightforward, but this is where it all gets a bit murky . . .

Let's start with the most famous story. The first phrase to be heard on a telephone was Bell, in one room, saying to Watson, in another room, 'Mr Watson – come here – I want to see you.' Bell had done it, he had invented the telephone.

However, by 1876 both Alexander Graham Bell and an American engineer called Elisha Gray claimed to have invented the telephone. They both applied for a patent at the same time (Bell was actually one hour earlier). A patent is a legal document that tells the world who created a certain invention.

The problem was that Gray had been working on a similar device to Bell's at the same time. In fact, Gray had even demonstrated his device in public, months before Bell had tried to get a patent. To make matters worse, it seemed that Bell may have stolen some of Gray's ideas and used them to make his telephone.

Happily ever after?

The argument over who invented the telephone dragged on for years and years, with lots of court cases. In the meantime, Bell set up a company and started to sell his telephones all over the world. His company did well, making Bell a very rich man.

It has never been decided whether Bell or Gray is the true inventor of the telephone. Most people agree that Bell did most of the work. It also seems probable that Bell used some of Gray's ideas. Whether Bell did this on purpose or not, no one knows.

Bell continued to invent. In 1881 he invented the metal detector. In 1896 he helped invent the hydrofoil and even played a small part in the invention of the aeroplane.

Bell died in 1922, at the age of 75, and has gone down in history as one the great Scottish inventors.

John Logie Baird: Smarter than the Average Inventor

I am sure you all love the telephone, and might even be a bit partial to licking stamps, but – let's face it – TV rules!

John Logie Baird was born and grew up in Helensburgh, in Dunbartonshire. Now, before we get into his story, I don't want you to get all Alexander Graham Bell on me. Baird didn't invent television by himself. He never claimed this, I am not claiming this, and in fact no one has ever really claimed this. However, Baird is the one person who did more than any other person to make sure you can watch soap opera every night.

The one thing Baird was the first to do was to produce a 'live, moving, greyscale television image from reflected light'. That is, he was the first to produce black-and-white moving images. He did this with some clever electronics.

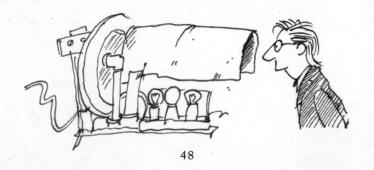

It was not all plain sailing for Baird. He worked at the problem of making a moving image for years. In 1923 he became ill and doctors suggested he move to the south coast of England where the fresh air might help him get better. He took their advice, and whilst in England he carried on experimenting, but after giving himself a massive electric shock (and, amazingly, surviving) his landlady insisted he find a new house. Baird moved to London and it was there that he made his breakthrough.

The first time Baird managed to produce a moving image was in his lab. He projected the head of a ventriloquist's dummy nicknamed 'Stooky Bill' onto a screen. Excited by what he had managed to do, Baird raced downstairs to find a live subject – 20-year-old office worker William Edward Taynton. This young man became the first ever person to appear on TV – now there's a fact to impress your mates with on a cold winter's night!

You might think that a serious scientist would want to show off his breakthrough to other serious scientists (or at least people in white coats). However, Baird chose to first demonstrate his moving image in a department store. That's right, TV was first showcased in 1925, in Selfridges in London.

John Logie Baird had a successful life as an inventor and lived out his final years in a house on Station Road, Bexhill-on-Sea, East Sussex. In 2007 this house was demolished and a block of flats built in its place. Today these flats are called 'Baird Court'.

3
Lighthouses

Scottish inventors have been inventing stuff for as long as Scotland has had hills (though they didn't invent the hills – obviously!). However, there was one time in the past when inventors were looked upon as heroes, a time when people didn't care about footballers and rappers and were, instead, impressed by the great minds of men and women. This was during the reign of Queen Victoria (well, it was also a little before, but let's not get our knickers in a twist).

We have seen how James Watt used steam-power, Thomas Telford built bridges, and John Logie Baird made moving pictures. Now let's shed some light on lighthouses (and other stuff).

Robert Stevenson:

Built a House on a Rock

Lighthouses might not seem like the most exciting things in the world, but when you consider the problems of building a huge torch on a rock in the middle of the sea, you can start to appreciate the skill of lighthouse builders.

Robert Stevenson grew up with lighthouses. His step-father worked in a company that made lighthouses, and Stevenson became his apprentice when only young. By 1796, though still only a young man, Stevenson was trusted to oversee some lighthouse building projects by himself. (Not literally by himself – that would have taken ages with all those bricks and giant light bulbs!)

Well done, lads

I could go on about Stevenson building this lighthouse and that lighthouse, but history tells us that one of Stevenson's successes matters above all others and that's the Bell Rock Lighthouse. This was a monster of a project. It was proposed that the lighthouse would be built on a small outcrop of rocks, Bell Rock, in the North Sea, 12 miles off the coast of Angus, in east Scotland. That's right, no nice easy roads, nothing but rocks, seaweed, and huge, freezing cold waves.

It was guessed that before the lighthouse was built as many as six ships were being wrecked on the Rock every single winter. And it wasn't the first time someone had tried to build a lighthouse there. Way back in the 1300s the Abbot of Arbroath had paid for the construction of a tower with a large bell that would warn off passing ships – more a bellhouse than a lighthouse. The bell was stolen by pirates shortly after the tower was built.

In 1804 the British warship HMS *York* was sunk after hitting the Bell Rock. The government got all we-need-a-lighthouse and Stevenson came to their rescue. In 1807 he gathered 60 men and set out for the Bell Rock.

The men lived on a ship moored alongside the Bell Rock. For 20 hours each day Stevenson and his men were hard at work, despite the fact that some days the sea would rise up and completely cover the Rock. Their first job was to build a wooden shelter, with enough room for 15 men to live inside. Once the winter months set in the weather was so bad it was too dangerous for his men to remain at Bell Rock and, by the winter of 1807, the wooden building was the only thing that had been built.

Spring 1808 saw the men return, but more bad weather followed and the Rock was battered by many storms. The

Right, Tam, it's your turn to go and wash the dishes.

men only managed 80 hours of work in total that summer. To add to their misery, a young man was killed after being knocked unconscious and washed into the sea. By the winter of 1808, the lighthouse was still not built.

The lighthouse wasn't completed until 1811. Stevenson used more than 2,500 huge blocks of stone to construct it, each of which had to be sailed by boat from the shore. Many people believed the lighthouse would be washed away in the first big storm. However, just months before the lighthouse was due to open a fierce seven-hour storm struck. Though one of the workmen was washed away and drowned, the lighthouse remained in place.

It is still there today, surviving two centuries of storms and even a helicopter crashing into it in 1955. Bell Rock Lighthouse is a flashing beacon to a great Scottish inventor.

Thomas Stevenson: Like Father Like Son

As far as lighthouse building is concerned, Robert Stevenson is a true Scottish hero. In fact, he might be the all-time-best-Scottish-lighthouse-builder, had his son, Thomas, not jumped in on the act. (I don't think there is an award for the all-time-best-Scottish-lighthouse-builder, but if there were then a Stevenson would win.)

Thomas Stevenson was brought up on lighthouses – well, not literally, he didn't actually live on a lighthouse. His dad built lighthouses for a living, and from an early age all he knew was lighthouses. It is therefore no surprise to learn that when Thomas grew up, he also became a lighthouse designer.

It took Stevenson's dad four years to build the lighthouse at Bell Rock. So how many lighthouses do you think Thomas Stevenson managed to knock up in his lifetime? Three, five, ten . . . ? Here's the answer:

Whalsay Skerries, Out Skerries, Muckle Flugga, Davaar, Ushenish, South Rona, Kyleakin, Ornsay, Sound of Mull, Cantick Head, Bressay, Rhuvaal, Corran Point, Fladda, McArthur's Head, St Abb's Head, Butt of Lewis, Holborn Head, Monach Islands, Skervuile, Auskerry,

Lochindaal, Scurdie Ness, Stoer Head, Dubh Artach, Turnberry Point, Chicken Rock, Lindisfarne, Fidra, Oxcar and Ailsa Craig.

That's 31 lighthouses . . . count 'em . . . 31! (Though I think the Butt of Lewis should count double!)

Thomas Drummond: Lighting the Light

Building a lighthouse is one thing but lighting it is another. Actually, now I think about it, building a lighthouse on a tiny rock, miles from the shore, is a tiny bit more difficult than inventing a light, but anyway . . . Our next Scot, Thomas Drummond, was the man whose new lighting system for lighthouses would have helped to save lives.

When Stevenson set out to build the Bell Rock lighthouse, the light in the top was nothing more than a huge candle made out of whale oil, surrounded by mirrors to make the whole thing a bit brighter. Better than nothing, but not great!

In the 1820s Goldsworthy Gurney (now there's a great name) invented a new type of lighting called Limelight (he stole the idea from a guy called Robert Hare, but shhh!). The science was simple. A light was created by an oxyhydrogen flame being directed on calcium oxide to produce a combination of incandescence and candoluminescence. Sorry, did I say it was simple? I meant complicated. In essence, a flame was used to heat a block of calcium (the same stuff bones and teeth are made from) and the light produced was super-bright.

The light became famous for being used in theatres, which is where the phrase 'in the limelight' comes from. In 1825 Thomas Drummond, our hero, saw another scientist giving a demonstration of the light. Drummond immediately realised he could make a few quid out of it, copied it, and made a new light called the Drummond Light.

By 1829 Drummond was experimenting with the lights in a number of lighthouses. For a time it looked like Drummond was on to a winner, but he soon hit problems. Though his lights were bright, they were very expensive. In the end the Drummond Light wasn't really used in that many lighthouses. Though it was much brighter than the whole candle-and-mirror affair, it was just too expensive. The Drummond Light was soon snuffed out by the arrival of much safer and cheaper electrical lights.

James Blyth: Full of Wind

I reckon Thomas Drummond was pretty chuffed with his oxyhydrogen flame, but James Blyth could light stuff up with wind (and I don't mean the kind of wind you are thinking about, no trouser wind here, thank you very much).

James Blyth was born in Marykirk, Kincardineshire, on 4 April 1839. He studied mathematics in Edinburgh and then in 1880 he moved to Glasgow to teach. He became obsessed with wind and how it could be used to generate electricity.

In 1887 Blyth built a huge windmill in his back garden. As it turned in the wind, the windmill powered a generator, which converted the energy to electricity. This electricity was then used to power the lights in the house. This meant that Blyth's house was the first in the world to be powered by wind-generated electricity. Blyth improved the design of the windmill and in the end it worked for 25 years. Our hero offered the extra electricity to be used to light the streetlights outside his house. The local council refused, saying electricity was the 'work of the Devil'!

Blyth's windmill did have one problem. It had no brake. This meant that when the wind blew hard the windmill spun faster and faster. Great, until a storm comes along and you are stuck with the super-fast Windmill of Death in your back garden!

Blyth designed another windmill, this time with a brake, and this was used at Montrose Lunatic Asylum.

4

Food

It is no secret that Scots love food. Building bridges, constructing lighthouses and generating electricity with wind may be impressive, but, to be honest, I love a good bag of chips. We can't take a tour of famous Scottish inventors without looking at a few that focused on food. And so, in honour of the Scottish belly, let's begin.

Barbara Gilmour: The Cheese Witch

During the 1660s the whole of the British Isles was in a bit of a mess and it was dangerous to have religious beliefs that differed from whoever was in power. Barbara Gilmour felt she wasn't safe and fled to Ireland to avoid people in Scotland who didn't agree with her religious beliefs. Whilst in Ireland she learned how to make cheese. She eventually felt it was safe to return to her home in Dunlop, East Ayrshire, and she brought with her the recipe for a new type of cheese. This became known as Dunlop Cheese (this is not the same Dunlop that made the tyres – he would have made horrible cheese, all rubbery and full of air!).

Back then you couldn't make cheese by using milk straight from a cow (up until this point cheese could only be made if some of the fat from the whole milk was removed first). So when Gilmour started making lovely cheese from whole milk the locals reacted in the only way possible – they accused her of being a witch. Luckily Gilmour was not a witch, though she was a wizard in the kitchen! (Wow, that's a bad joke. I bet the publisher won't let me keep that one in. If you see a blank space here you know why.)

The secret to making Dunlop Cheese was to use a cheese press. This is a machine used to squeeze all the liquid out of the cheese. It is said that Barbara Gilmour's original cheese press can still be found at her farm in Dunlop. It looks a bit like a big stone cupboard. The cheese would be placed at the bottom and a big stone placed on top to squeeze out all the liquid. We can't be sure that this really is her original cheese press, however. Gilmour died in 1732 and the date on the cheese press says 1760!

By the time Gilmour died, she – or, more precisely, her cheese – was famous all over the country. When they buried her they made her gravestone out of a huge piece of cheese, but it was eaten by badgers. (That's a lie, sorry!)

Janet Keiller: A Boat-load of Oranges

It is 1797 and Janet Keiller is not a happy wife. Janet and James Keiller live in Dundee. James Keiller is a business-man who couldn't resist the temptation to buy a ship-load of oranges when they were offered to him at a super-low price. However, when he checks his new purchase he finds that they are not fresh and he will not be able to sell them in the market. So he does what all good husbands do and asks his wife for advice.

Janet Keiller has a brainwave. She will use the oranges to make orange jam.

This was not new, as recipes for orange jam already existed, but what Janet did that was different was add the rind (the skin) to the recipe. The new jam was a success and marmalade was born.

The Keillers went on to have a huge success with their marmalade. They set up the world's first marmalade factory and exported pots of the sticky stuff to countries far and wide.

So next time someone asks you if you'd like to buy a boat-load of oranges, you know what to say.

Alexander Grant: He Takes the Biscuit

We can pretend that inventors like James Watt and Thomas Telford are our favourite inventors, but I suspect when you hear about Alexander Grant, he might just top your Top Five Favourite Scottish Inventors list.

In 1890 Robert McVitie and his father opened a shop on Rose Street, Edinburgh. In the basement of the shop was a bakery where Robert experimented with cakes and other goodies. The bakery soon became more popular than the shop, and the business went from strength to strength. By 1875 the company had grown so big that they had to build their own factory on the outskirts of Edinburgh.

Enter Alexander Grant. He joined the company in 1887 and worked his way up the ranks. Eventually he was trusted with making and designing his own products.

Now, this is the big moment, do you know what Grant invented, using a secret recipe, a recipe that is still used today? No?

The digestive biscuit!

That's right. Grant invented the king of biscuits – the digestive (he didn't invent the infinitely superior chocolate version that came along in 1925, but let's not let that get in the way of a good story). Do you know why it's called the 'digestive' biscuit? It is all to do with the addition of sodium bicarbonate, which is said to help with digestion. However, if you check out a packet of digestive biscuits sold in America you will find the following notice: 'The ingredients in this biscuit do not contain any substances that assist digestion.' Their laws about what you can include on the labels for food are pretty strict.

So next time your teacher is banging on about great Scottish inventors, don't forget to raise your hand and confidently point out that Alexander Grant should be at the top of the list.

5

Warfare

We have established that Scots love to invent, they love to build stuff and they love to eat. Scots from the past were also famous for one other thing – fighting. From Calgacus who fought the Romans, to Douglas Haig who led the British army in the First World War, we see great Scots doing great things on the battlefield. It will therefore not come as a surprise when I tell you that many of the great Scottish inventors liked to invent weapons.

Robert Melville: Don't Get Too Close

Robert Melville was born on 12 October 1723 at Monimail in Fife. He was from a famous and rich family and studied medicine at both Edinburgh and Glasgow universities. He then joined the army and fought in many battles including the Battle of Fontenoy in Europe and the Battle of Culloden in Scotland. He spent the later part of his life in the Caribbean, fighting to capture islands from the French. In 1771 he returned to Scotland.

All of this is well and good. Melville was a brave soldier and a great general. However, what interests us is what he did when he retired. Most people who retire like to take up golf, write letters to the local newspaper about the price of soup and start wearing comfortable slippers. But Melville

was not a golf-playing, letter-writing or slipper-wearing old bloke. He had a much better plan – he was going to invent a new type of cannon!

His cannon was designed to be used on huge galleon warships – the ones with lots of sails, bristling with guns. Melville noticed that all the guns being used were really good for shooting at long range but a bit rubbish when the battle got close-up and dirty. He invented a cannon called a cannonade that had a very short barrel. This meant that when fired, the cannonball would not go as far. However, it did have two big advantages – it was quick to reload and it was much lighter than a normal cannon. This meant ships had a choice. Have a few normal cannons that could fire a long way, or have lots of cannonades that couldn't fire as far, but could do more damage if fighting up close.

In the end, the cannonade never really took off. A few experimental warships, like HMS *Glatton* and HMS *Rainbow*, tried using the guns but the British navy decided that longer-range and more accurate guns were the way forward.

There is actually a little twist to the story. Though it was Melville who invented the cannonade, it was a Scottish company called Carron who made some money out of it. What happened was Charles Gascoigne (whose dad had fought at the Battle of Culloden with Melville) copied the design for the cannonade and made it a bit better. Gascoigne was not a nice bloke and the British army and navy didn't really trust him. This is one of the reasons that the cannonade was never very widely used.

Patrick Ferguson: Breaching the Problem

Our gun-loving hero was born in Edinburgh in 1744. His story isn't that different from Melville's, the cannonade guy. Ferguson joined the army and fought in Europe until he picked up a leg injury. He returned to Scotland before popping over to the Caribbean. All those months on board ships took their toll and our hero's leg injury was soon playing up. In agony, Ferguson had no choice but to return to Scotland. Much like Melville, Ferguson was not the type to retire, and seeing as he had time on his hands he decided to invent a new type of rifle.

To understand just why Ferguson should be remembered as a great Scottish inventor, we need to know a bit about guns. At the time Ferguson joined the army, soldiers were using a type of gun called a musket. This looked like a modern rifle but had one big difference – the inside of the gun barrel was made of smooth metal. This meant that the bullet would come out of the gun straight but would fly off in random directions, making shooting inaccurate. The gun was also 'muzzle-loading', which meant the bullet and gunpowder had to be stuffed down the barrel of the gun before it could be fired.

Ferguson started to use a different type of gun. This was called a rifle. Rather than having a smooth barrel, this had grooves carved into the inside which made the bullet spin when it was fired. This meant that the bullet was much more accurate and could go much further. The big problem Ferguson faced was that rifles still had to be loaded by pushing stuff down the muzzle, and this was slow, messy and dangerous.

Our hero took a big step forward when he invented the 'breach-loading' rifle. It was known as the Ferguson Rifle and it had a clever design that allowed part of the gun, just above the trigger, to be opened. The gunpowder and bullet could then be added, and the gun closed and fired. It was a much faster way of loading the gun than having to stuff everything in the end and poke it down with a long stick.

It looked like Ferguson had made a breakthrough. But the gun never took off. It was used in the American Wars of Independence, which saw American and British troops fighting in America, but the problem was that troops often got the bullets mixed up and tried to push the wrong bullets into the Ferguson Rifle. An even bigger problem was that the rifle was expensive and very slow to make. Only 100 were produced in six months.

On 7 October 1780, the American and British armies met at the famous Battle of Kings Mountain in America. Patrick Ferguson fought in this battle, but was shot from

his horse. He fell to the ground, but his foot became entangled in his stirrup. His horse dragged him over the battle lines to the American side. He might have survived, but he decided that although he was helplessly tied to a horse and on his back, he would take the opportunity to shoot an American general with his pistol. After the battle, Ferguson's mutilated body was found with eight bullet holes riddling his dead corpse.

James Paris Lee: A Bolt out of the Blue

Our next gun-toting Scottish inventor is a guy called James Paris Lee. He was born in 1831, just over fifty years after poor Patrick Ferguson was drilled full of musket balls. Lee lived in Hawick, in the Scottish Borders, but moved to Canada when he was just five years old.

Lee was not a normal kid – he was fascinated by guns. In fact, he built his first gun, aged just 12. It was from a kit and didn't work very well. He became obsessed with making better and more reliable weapons.

It was no surprise to anyone that Lee grew up to become a gun-maker, in fact he had a factory and everything. Guns and bullets had moved on from Ferguson's day. No longer did the firer have to load the gunpowder and bullet separately. These were now combined in one single brass cartridge. When the gun fired, the bullet would leave the end of the gun and the hot, empty cartridge would be ejected out the side.

Lee's idea was to develop a new way of getting the cartridge into the rifle. Before Lee's invention each cartridge would have to be loaded by hand. Lee invented a special system that allowed the firer to pull a bolt that would lift the cartridge from a magazine (a small metal box holding the bullets) into the gun. The result was that the gun could be fired more quickly.

Our hero died in 1904 but his new rifle, called a 'bolt action' rifle, was used in the First and Second World Wars by both British and American armies.

The Ghillie Suit:
Or How to Win at Hide and Seek

Let's finish our look at Scottish inventors who invented stuff to kill people, with an invention that is designed to stop you being killed.

The ghillie suit is a posh name for a camouflage jacket. It's really that simple – a big jacket with camouflage pattern and perhaps some twigs and leaves attached to make the person wearing it blend into the landscape. The name comes from *gille*, the Gaelic word for 'servant'. The jacket was first used by Scottish hunters in the Highlands.

In 1900 Simon Fraser, the 14th Lord Lovat and the 23rd chief of Clan Fraser, created a new unit in the British army. They were known as the Lovat Scouts. The idea was to produce a group of men who could blend into the battle-field, living off the land and attacking the enemy from behind their lines. Major Frederick Russell Burnham, the man who helped set up the Lovat Scouts, described the soldiers as 'half wolf and half rabbit'. Burnham was a great friend of Robert Baden-Powell and they fought together in the Boer War in Africa. The two men often discussed starting an organisation to help young boys. After the war Baden-Powell set up the Boy Scouts, though many argue that it was actually Burnham's idea.

The Lovat Scouts were the first people to use the ghillie suit in combat. They wore it when they were fighting in Africa. Today, the person you are most likely to see wearing a ghillie suit (or not see, if you know what I mean) is a sniper. Each sniper makes his own ghillie suit – it can take weeks of building and modifying the camouflage to make snipers virtually invisible on the battlefield.

6
Crime

Before you get carried away thinking Scottish inventors are all do-gooders trying to make the world a better place (or at least a place with better weapons), here's one great Scot who spent his time thinking up devious – and often painful – ways to torture and kill people. Oh, and one who tried to catch criminals . . .

James Douglas: Liked a Nice Clean Chop

Chopping off people's heads is not easy. You see, the neck is such a small target and all the bone, muscle and skin get in the way.

In medieval times a common execution tool was a large axe, but it was difficult to use and often missed the neck. It was not uncommon for poor victims to have to wait for three or four chops before their heads popped off.

The Scots had always been ahead of the game when it came to beheading and they liked to use a nice long sword rather than an axe. The sword was more stable, took fewer blows and even had a couple of handy grooves in the blade to let the blood run freely.

One Scottish inventor who revolutionised the art of chopping off people's heads was James Douglas, 4th Earl of Morton. He was regent of Scotland in the 1550s (this meant whilst Scotland tried to decide which king or queen should be on the throne, he ran the country). The story goes that whilst travelling from London to Edinburgh, James Douglas stopped over at Halifax in the north of England. There he witnessed the execution of a criminal, using a wooden machine, a kind of guillotine, known as the Halifax Gibbet. Douglas was very pleased with what he saw, writing that he was impressed by 'its clean work'.

When he returned to Edinburgh he paid for a similar machine to be built and it became known as the Scottish Maiden.

The machine had a wooden frame. The victim would rest his head and exposed neck at the bottom of the frame, whilst the blade waited at the top. The blade was kept in place by a peg. The peg was attached to a rope and the rope was attached to a lever. The executioner would then pull the lever, releasing the blade and cleanly whipping off the head of the poor criminal.

Now, this is all pretty gruesome, but those medieval executioners had a real sense of humour. Let's say you had been found guilty of stealing some sheep. They could just pull the lever in the usual manner, which would be messy but no real fun. They liked to get creative. Instead they could get a sheep, tie the rope to the animal, smack it on the bum and send it running off. The rope would release the peg and – whoosh – no more head. In fact, this is just what the Scottish executioners would do if your crime involved an animal – they would try to use that animal to chop off your head!

Before we leave James Douglas and his Maiden, I have one more juicy fact. In medieval Scotland, kings and regents tended to come to a bloody end, and James was no exception. In 1579 Douglas was accused of helping to plot the murder of Lord Darnley. He was found guilty and sentenced to death. The judge couldn't resist insisting that he was killed by his very own invention – the Scottish Maiden.

The execution took place in Edinburgh and Douglas' body was left headless by the wooden frame for a full day afterwards. His head was popped on a spike and displayed outside Tolbooth Prison in Edinburgh.

In the end, Douglas' head and body were reunited and buried . . . well . . . we are not entirely sure that's true. Legend says he is buried in Greyfriars Kirkyard. It is said that a small sandstone post with the letters 'J.E.M.' marks the grave. There are two problems with this. The first is that his name was James Douglas – that's J.D. not J.E.M. The second is that in 1595, years after Douglas' burial, all stones were removed from Greyfriars. But, hey, let's not let the facts get in the way of a good story.

Henry Faulds: The Man with the Fingers

Not all Scots were obsessed with killing criminals, some just wanted to make sure the right man was locked up. Enter Henry Faulds and his fingers.

Faulds was born in Beith, North Ayrshire, but went to school and university in Glasgow. When he left university he became a missionary and travelled to India and Japan. It was whilst in Japan that Faulds first became interested in fingers, or finger*prints* to be more exact.

The year was 1874, and Faulds was helping out at an archaeological dig in Japan. He noticed that many of the ancient clay fragments that they were digging up were still marked with the fingerprints of the last person to handle them all those centuries ago. This got Faulds thinking – could fingerprints be used to identify a person?

Our hero took to examining the fingerprints of every person he met and within weeks was convinced that each individual's fingerprints were unique (which was true). Armed with this fact he went to the Japanese police to tell them about his new way of identifying criminals. The police weren't convinced.

Shortly after approaching the police, the hospital at which Faulds was working was broken into and items were stolen. The police arrested a member of staff who Faulds knew was innocent. Faulds came to his rescue. He compared the fingerprints from the crime scene with those of the arrested man. They were different and the police agreed to let the man go free.

Sadly, this is where Faulds' impact on history ends. He returned to Britain in 1886 and tried to convince the English police to use fingerprints, but they refused. Faulds even went to Charles Darwin and asked him to help. He also refused.

It might not have been Faulds that convinced the police to start using fingerprints to catch bad guys . . . but he did get the ball rolling. Sir Francis Galton (another mate of Charles Darwin) was inspired by Faulds to prove that no two fingerprints were identical. After this, police forces from all over the world slowly started to collect fingerprints. However, it wasn't until 1902, in France, that the first person was sent to prison because of fingerprint evidence.

7

Medicine

Scotland is great at producing doctors. You can look back as far as medicine has been practised to see Scottish doctors inventing new treatments to help cure the ill. Here are just a few examples of great inventing Scottish doctors . . .

James Lind:

Liked to Grow Stuff on Blankets

Before the days of ships driven by engines, the only way to travel long distances over the sea was using sail power. Though sailing ships could cross the globe, they were slow and sailors would be stuck on their ship for months or even years. One of the main problems for sailors, apart from having to live in close quarters with other smelly sailors, was that they had to find space on the ship for all the food and water they needed for their voyage. This meant that fresh vegetables and meat were very rare.

Many sailors would become ill with a disease called scurvy. This was caused by a lack of an important vitamin – vitamin C. The disease would start with spots on the skin, painful gums and nose bleeds. As it got worse the victim would get more spots, become pale, feel depressed and have no energy. Eventually the spots would become open wounds and their

teeth would fall out. Then they dropped dead!

This is where our hero James Lind comes onto the scene. Lind was born in Edinburgh in 1716. He trained as a doctor before joining the navy. By 1747 he had become the doctor on the HMS *Salisbury*. Lind saw that scurvy was a big problem and set about trying to find a cure.

He split the crew of the ship into six groups and gave them the following things to eat or drink as well as their normal rations:

Group 1: Cider
Group 2: Sulphuric acid
Group 3: Vinegar
Group 4: Sea water
Group 5: Two oranges and a lemon
Group 6: Barley water

Lind noticed that the sailors eating the fruit showed no sign of scurvy.

Our experimenting doctor continued to offer helpful tips for sailors at sea. He suggested that ships grow water-

cress on wet blankets, and in 1775 the whole of the British navy was given watercress seeds. Though Lind did actually find the cure for scurvy, which turned out to be eating citrus fruit like oranges, he never understood just how important his research would turn out to be. It was Lind's work that allowed other doctors to teach sailors the best foods to eat to avoid scurvy.

James Baird: Look into My Eyes

In 1841 Scottish doctor James Baird went to a show to watch a man called Charles Lafontaine. It was a display of what was then called mesmerism. This was where one person would put another into a trance and make them do silly stuff (you know, like eat a raw onion or pretend to be a chicken).

Baird was prepared to dismiss mesmerism as fake, but after seeing the act numerous times he became convinced that there must be a scientific explanation. Baird began experimenting to find out how it was done. He persuaded his wife, a friend and a servant to stare at an object for a very long time, and found he could bring on a trance (a bit like watching *Eastenders*!).

Our hero determined that the trance was a type of sleep and called it 'hypno', after Hypnos, the Greek god of sleep and master of dreams. By 1847 hypnosis was all the rage. Baird hated the name hypnosis (he didn't think it sounded scientific enough) and wanted to call it 'monoideism' instead. But it was too late and 'monoideism' was a rubbish name. 'Hypnosis' stuck and Baird went down in history.

Hypnosis turned out to be much more than just a party trick. It is still used today to help people with phobias (extreme fears of things like spiders) and even to break habits like smoking.

James Young Simpson: A Party Animal

James Simpson was born in Bathgate, West Lothian, in 1811. It was clear from a young age that he was very clever, so he was sent to Edinburgh University to train to be a doctor. He graduated at the age of 18, but was too young actually to practise as a doctor and had to wait until he was 20 before he could start.

Our hero's real interest was in midwifery (that's babies being born). He saw that birth was very painful for the mothers and he wanted to find a way to ease the pain. Simpson became fascinated with anaesthetics – chemicals that get rid of pain. He was not the first doctor to think about anaesthetics and there were actually a few chemicals that had already been tried. The first was nitrous oxide – laughing gas to you and me. This worked OK but was

difficult to give to patients and could be dangerous. Later, a chemical called ether was used. This smelly liquid would cause the patient to fall unconscious, allowing the doctor to do whatever painful procedure he needed to do. At first it seemed that ether would be the answer, but it turned out that it was also dangerous, damaging the lungs of the poor patients.

In 1847 Simpson and two friends, Dr Keith and Dr Duncan, started to have anaesthetic parties. They would gather around a table and sniff in various chemicals, looking for ones that might knock them out. One night Simpson turned up with a bottle of chloroform. All three doctors took a big sniff and found that they became all giggly and playful. Then suddenly they all collapsed, only to come round the next morning.

Simpson knew he was on to something and like all good, mad, doctors he tried it out on his family. His niece was called and when she fell asleep after taking a big snifter, Simpson was delighted. He is recorded to have said, 'I am an angel!' It turned out that all three doctors (and the niece) had been pretty lucky. If you sniff in a small amount of chloroform nothing happens, but if you honk up too much you keel over and die. It was pure chance that all four experimenters inhaled the correct amount.

Chloroform was quickly seen as a miracle cure to pain in childbirth. Simpson used it on his patients, easing the pain as they pushed out the baby. In 1853 Queen Victoria used chloroform during the delivery of Prince Leopold (we don't know if she was amused or not).

John Scott Haldane: The Canary Killer!

Some Scottish inventors are serious and boring characters, some are exciting and eccentric, some are just plain mad. I think it is safe to say that John Scott Haldane was a little bit mad.

Haldane was born in Edinburgh in 1860 and trained to become a doctor at Edinburgh University. Now, all doctors have their special interests, parts of medicine that fascinate them and guide their thinking and experiments. Haldane was obsessed with poison! Luckily he was interested in

finding out how poison worked so he could save people's lives, rather than so he could murder his patients and bury them in his garden!

Our hero was particularly interested in poisonous gases.

In order to work out how to stop these gases being deadly, Haldane needed to know how they worked on the human body. He came up with a solution – he would poison himself! Haldane built a special sealed chamber in which he could sit. He would then pump in poisonous gases and record how it felt to be poisoned (I told you he was mad), though he was careful not to give himself so much poison that he dropped dead (he wasn't THAT mad!).

Poisonous gases were a huge threat to people who worked in mines because gases would collect underground. Haldane came up with two things to help miners avoid pockets of poisonous gas. The first was the invention of a lamp with a small flame. The flame grew or shrank in the presence of different gases, giving the miners an early warning of any danger. The second was the introduction of small yellow canaries. These birds were very sensitive to carbon monoxide, a gas that can be deadly to humans. The bird was carried in a small cage by the miners. If the bird suddenly choked and dropped dead the miners knew the carbon monoxide levels were high and it wasn't safe to go further – though it was too late for the poor bird!

Another of Haldane's notable inventions was a gas mask used in World War I. When it was discovered that the Germans were using chlorine-based gases as weapons, Haldane knew he had the solution. His gas mask was nothing more than a strip of material soaked in a chemical that would neutralise the poisonous chlorine gas. A soldier would wrap the material around his face and eyes, keeping them safe. Do you know what soldiers could do if they didn't have a mask? Well, the chemical that neutralises chlorine is called ammonia and a good source of ammonia is urine (that's wee to you and me). So a quick widdle on a cloth and, hey presto, a makeshift gas mask! Not very pretty, but pretty effective.

8

The Weird and Wonderful

Scottish inventors have created great and earth-shattering stuff. After all, where would we be today without television, telephones and, of course, mail delivered by hot-air balloons? However, some Scottish inventors were a little bit odd and liked to invent things that were, let's face it, a bit weird. Here's a quick look . . .

Alexander Cummings:
Flushed with Success

It is a common mistake to think that Thomas Crapper invented the first flush toilet (though I wish with all my heart it was true). In fact, the first person to invent a system for flushing away all those number 1s and 2s was Scottish inventor Alexander Cummings.

He was born in Edinburgh in 1733 and was a mathematician and watchmaker. He moved to London as a young man and opened a business on Bond Street. In 1775 Cummings registered a patent for what was to become the first flush toilet. However, before we get carried away we need to mention Sir John Harington.

In 1596 Harington invented what he called a water closet. Up to this point people had pooed in a bucket and chucked the contents into the street (yes, really!). Harington's idea was to fill a big container with water, then once the job had been done, a lever was pulled to release the water. The container would then need to be refilled. Harington actually built a water closet like this for Elizabeth I of England, but she refused to use it because it was too noisy.

slurpsh!
gurgle!
splosh!
slurp!
gloop!

It seems that Harington had done all the work, so why all the fuss over Cummings?

Cummings spotted the problem with Harington's design – having to refill the container by hand after each flush. Cummings invented a system that stored a reservoir of water above the toilet. When the toilet was flushed the reservoir would open, automatically refilling, ready for the next smelly visit.

James Ballantyne Hannay: Making Money

Let's say you were a Victorian gentleman and you wanted a nice new diamond for your lady wife. You could pop down to the jewellers and pay a big wad of cash for a nice shiny stone. Or you could travel all the way to the diamond mines in South Africa (dodging Zulus and Boers on the way) and dig up your own shiny stone. James Ballantyne Hannay was not a man to buy diamonds or dig them up; instead he invented a way to MAKE diamonds.

Hannay was born in Glasgow in 1855. He was a brilliant chemist and invented a number of new dyes. But forget that boring stuff because we're talking about shiny, sparkly DIAMONDS!

In 1880 Hannay published a paper that described how he had made a diamond in his lab. He explained that he had mixed paraffin, bone oil and lithium until red hot, and then sealed the mixture in iron tubes. When everything had cooled he opened the tubes and out popped a diamond. Well, not an actual diamond, but what Hannay had created was millions of tiny diamond particles – more diamond dust than diamond ring.

The thing is that Hannay was on to something big. The process he used was the start of many experiments, by many scientists, eventually to produce what we today call synthetic diamonds. You see, it is possible to make a diamond in the lab, but jewellers don't class these as real diamonds – the spoilsports!

Charles Macintosh: A Mac with a Mac

The last of our Scottish inventors is a guy who tackled the one problem that all Scots face – the rain.

Charles Macintosh was born in Glasgow in 1766. Macintosh started his working life in an office but soon became fascinated with chemicals. He taught himself chemistry and in 1797 even set up his own successful factory. He was a non-stop inventor and over his lifetime invented loads of stuff, including a type of printing, a method for dyeing cloth blue, a way to bleach material, a way to preserve citric acid during ocean voyages (remember the scurvy?), a yeast (we use it to make bread) production process and loads of things involving iron and steel. However, the first thing Mac is remembered for is his mac.

In 1820 he was playing with some chemicals when he stumbled on a way of sealing a layer of rubber between two layers of cloth. The new material was very waterproof, so ideal for making coats. This new type of coat quickly became known as a macintosh or a mac. Our hero knew a good thing when he saw it and quickly set up factories in Glasgow and Manchester to make the material. He died in 1843, a happy (and very rich) man knowing he had helped thousands of people stay dry. And because no great Scottish inventor has come up with an invention to stop the rain, macs remain as popular today as they were in the 1800s.